THE POWER OF
faith

How God Changed My Life
And Will Change Yours

TRINA L. HOUSE, LPC-S

THE POWER OF FAITH
Copyright © 2022 Trina L. House

All rights reserved.
Published by Publish Your Gift®
An imprint of Purposely Created Publishing Group, LLC

No part of this book may be reproduced, distributed or transmitted in any form by any means, graphic, electronic, or mechanical, including photocopy, recording, taping, or by any information storage or retrieval system, without permission in writing from the publisher, except in the case of reprints in the context of reviews, quotes, or references.

Scriptures marked BRG are taken from Blue Red and Gold Letter Edition™. Copyright © 2012 by BRG Bible Ministries. Used by permission. All rights reserved.

Scriptures marked NIV are taken from the New International Version®. Copyright © 1973, 1978, 1984, 2011 by Biblica, Inc.™. All rights reserved.

Scriptures marked KJV are taken from the Holy Bible, King James Version. All rights reserved.

Scriptures marked GW are taken from God's Word Translation. Copyright © 1995, 2003, 2013, 2014, 2019, 2020 by God's Word to the Nations Mission Society. All rights reserved.

Scriptures marked NKJV are taken from the New King James Version®. Copyright © 1982 by Thomas Nelson. All rights reserved.

Scriptures marked ESV are taken from English Standard Version®. Copyright © 2001 by Crossway, a publishing ministry of Good News Publishers. All rights reserved.

Printed in the United States of America
ISBN: 978-1-64484-587-5 (print)
ISBN: 978-1-64484-588-2 (ebook)

Special discounts are available on bulk quantity purchases by book clubs, associations and special interest groups. For details email: sales@publishyourgift.com or call (888) 949-6228.
For information log on to www.PublishYourGift.com

To Rickey

Thank you for teaching me about God, love, commitment, joy, and strength. Thank you for being my superman.

Table of Contents

Foreword ix

Chapter 1: Awakening 1

Chapter 2: Mother's Message 11

Chapter 3: The Complexity of Men 23

Chapter 4: Self-Esteem and Friendship 41

Chapter 5: Relationship Day One 57

Chapter 6: My Son the Blessing 67

Chapter 7: The Pattern of Marriage 75

Chapter 8: Love and Power in the Church 81

Chapter 9: Wealth and Riches 101

Chapter 10: Continuous Learning 111

About the Author 119

Foreword

You know those periods of life when you're in a stage where everything is going well and you feel like you got it all figured out only to have what seems like an earthquake come and shake the very foundation you've built—the career, relationship, friends, and your faith walk?

I remember when I finally got a groove in my business around 2016, I was happily dating a man I still love, and I was jet-setting with the best of them only to learn one day just after my conference that my father had his left leg amputated from a condition called neuropathy. I was devastated by the news, but I was more devastated that my mother didn't tell me before it happened.

If I had to describe it, I felt like I had been gut punched on my wedding day by the love of my life! I thought, *But things are going so well. Why now, Lord?!*

As I was getting "used to" my father's new normal, my life started back on the uptick. Then, boom! My father was diagnosed with lung cancer. Then came the chemo treatments, phantom pains in what used to be his leg, and a new set of concerns about his life. My mother and I took the responsibility to support in any way that we could.

I was unfamiliar with how to handle the duality. How could I live in my purpose of helping women entrepreneurs *and* be sad that my father was dealing with some of his greatest challenges? The burden of both of those experiences had me feeling like my heart and mind were yo-yoing every day for a couple of years.

What kept me going was my spiritual beliefs and the faith I had that this was the path I was meant to walk. I learned to accept what *is* instead of wishing things were different. I had to truly accept and own my journey.

This amazing book is about the belief that you can live in both worlds at the same time. The knowing that no matter what comes in your path, you can evolve with it, be burdened by it, and still choose to grow from it. Moving in uncertain-certainty. Uncertain about the days ahead yet certain that everything will work out for your greater good.

I met Trina nearly ten years ago when I lived in Oklahoma City. You don't even understand how amazing this woman is! As her coach (and internet auntie) I have watched her experience her marriage almost falling apart, her stepping into full entrepreneurship and taking risks her peers were afraid to take, and then her having an aneurysm during the pandemic. I remember when Rickey (Trina's husband) called me when she had the aneurysm to let me know exactly what was going on. The prayers and support that Trina had while she was in the coma had to be the size of Texas—friends, family, online business friends, and strangers that never even met her held her full recovery in prayer.

While we were all in fear of the pandemic and losing our planet and our livelihood, she was being protected in the most seemingly bizarre way—safe "sleep"—unbothered by the chaos many of us were living. Again, the duality of it all. Feeling many different emotions at the same time about, well, everything.

I appreciate Trina's honesty and transparency as a woman of faith, a wife, a mother, and a business leader. She never hides the truth, her hard times, or her wins. That's the type of person you want to be connected to. Someone who shows real life—the duality of experiences that feel good and the circumstances that feel like the burden is too heavy to bear, only to learn that it's all a part of your God story.

The gift you'll get from absorbing these pages is knowing what true faith and belief looks like through

Trina's journey. You'll understand that your life has meaning beyond what you can see today. These pages are all the evidence you need to overcome any set of circumstances you may be experiencing right now. This book will prove that nothing can stop a person who is determined not to be stopped, not even being in a coma for weeks.

CHAPTER 1

Awakening

ORIGINS

I own a group therapeutic practice where we provide mental health services. We focus on helping youths, adults, and families overcome challenges such as anxiety, depression, grief, and loss. We work on all levels—cognitive, emotional, and holistic—in order to achieve lasting changes. For a time, life was pretty routine for me. Every morning, I would wake up, take my son to school, and go to the office. I would skip breakfast, though I would often make tea at the office and get to work. My typical daily roster consisted of a few clients. Aside from meeting with my clients, I would attend to various elements of my business, including checking on my contracted therapists and case managers. I made sure they had what they needed to see their clients, meet their supervision requirements, and practice solid reporting standards.

I was always thinking of ways to train my staff locally and abroad, and I also took time to explore my interests, as it relates to mental health and well-being, such as becoming a certified yogi. Mental health encompasses our emotional, psychological, and social well-being. It affects how we think, feel, and act; it also helps to determine how we handle stress, relate to others, and make healthy choices. Mental health is essential at every stage of life—childhood, adolescence, and adulthood.

After a typical afternoon, I would be off to pick up my son. Thoughts of dinner were next on the agenda as I supported my son with his homework. I seldom planned dinner; my husband is the better cook. Seriously! I would mostly order food, and dinner would typically end with me getting comfy for a few more hours, reading, and doing more work on the laptop.

In the spring of 2020, I was tasked with structuring appointments for my staff in the face of COVID-19. Children were a particular challenge; they are used to support that comes directly to their homes, but that couldn't happen anymore with the pandemic. Suddenly, I had to get my staff trained on virtual meetings and live therapy modalities, all via laptop. I wanted to make sure that my clients got what they needed.

My husband grew medical cannabis, and he was on his own schedule with business and sales meetings. On the evening of March 29, 2020, he was scheduled to attend a meeting, but he decided to cancel and come home.

Later that night, around 10:00 p.m., my thirteen-year-old son and I were watching a movie in the living room. I don't remember what we were watching; watching movies together is a normal thing that we do. At one point, I stood up and said, "I have a headache, but it's different. Something is wrong." My husband, for some reason, thought that I needed to cool down.

"Maybe you should take a shower," he suggested. I made my way to the restroom and sat on the toilet. My husband followed me and talked to me to keep me company. After a few minutes of watching me, he was set on a course of action: "I am taking you to the emergency room."

I remember leaning out of the car window and throwing up.

I remember the hospital's overflow tents set up outside to care for COVID-19 patients.

I remember people talking to me while I laid in a hospital bed, unable to respond to them.

My husband wanted to stay with me at the hospital but was forced to drop me off; he later told me what he had gone through. The hospital staff would not let him stay due to COVID-19 protocols, so he didn't find out my diagnosis until 6:00 a.m. the following morning. He was pissed; he is used to taking care of the family in multiple ways. As my superman, we are always together. That night, he didn't sleep. My son slept in the bed with him as they were both worried about me.

HOSPITALIZATION

The diagnosis was two brain aneurysms that ruptured. I wasn't the only one in my family to suffer a brain aneurysm. In 2007, my uncle broke down the door to my grandmother's home to find her lying on the floor in her dining room, debilitated. He and the rest of the family spent time with her at the hospital before she passed away.

I had high blood pressure, and I knew that I was at risk because of my genetics. But before that point, I had not put the two realities together in my mind to any degree that would motivate lifestyle changes. I had been diagnosed with high blood pressure years before my hospitalization. I was even prescribed medicine that I refused to take. I did not want to be a person who needed to take medication every day. And to be honest, I did not want the realities of illness, or the risk of impeding my progress or clouding my sense of self. As accomplished as I was in my life, career, and family, I wanted life on my own terms.

Instead of taking my prescribed medication, I hoped to benefit from herbs and homeopathic approaches, which I dabbled in without any consistent dedication. With high blood pressure, I probably should not have been eating the high sodium pickles I loved so much. (After my husband introduced them to me, I got in the habit of making and enjoying them often.) I maintained a full schedule and lived the life I wanted, including my diet, my way. I was not raised to eat healthily, and my husband had not learned that lesson either in his childhood home.

I was suffering the consequences.

I stayed in the hospital for a month. I now call the day I was released from the hospital my Awakening Birthday. Multiple changes resulted from the experience. My life is now more open after that brush with my mortality. I am no longer in a chrysalis as a caterpillar; I have emerged as a butterfly. The connections between diet, exercise, and health are now crystal clear to me. I take my medicine and watch my health inputs as well as my health outcomes.

My recovery, not to be cliché, was nothing short of a miracle. Subarachnoid hemorrhage (SAH) is bleeding into the space between the brain and the membranes that cover the brain. SAH requires immediate and urgent medical attention. After the first hemorrhage, about 46 percent of patients die. If the aneurysm is not repaired in time and a second hemorrhage occurs about 80 percent of patients die. A ruptured brain (aneurysm) is fatal in about 40 percent of cases. Of those who survive, about 66 percent suffer some permanent neurological deficit. Approximately 15 percent of people with a ruptured aneurysm die before reaching the hospital. Most of the deaths are due to rapid and massive brain injury from the initial bleeding. Doctors were excited that I could walk and function after such an event. I had to put in some work to recover my speech, mental processing, critical thinking, and attention-based skills, but my gross motor skills quickly and fully recovered. I have no drooping or balance issues at all.

ON GOD

My life has changed dramatically in the year since that incident. I feel like I died a year ago and was reborn as a totally different woman. While I continue learning about who the new me is, I do know two things: I know that I am trying my best to be an amazing wife and mother, and I know that God is real. The illness and risk that I feared came true, but God's love and care got me through. My husband is the reason I have learned what I have learned about God, and his family is an inspiration in many ways. For example, his great uncle is the bishop at the church we attend, New Dimensions Ministries, and my parents-in-law were married for twenty-five years until his mother's passing.

Not only do I rely on divine support, but I am also committed to doing my part for my own physical health as well as my general well-being. The path to glory is a clear, lifelong quest to focus on positivity. In the hospital, leading up to my Awakening Birthday, I focused on the positives. After learning all the lessons that I could from the experience, I cherished family and friends. I was on the path of progress and prosperity. After that experience, I also found myself more courageous and ready to face even my deepest fears.

I am now more open and more diligent with myself as a whole. I am more than a career, home, and list of achievements. I am emotion, mind, body, and spirit.

MY PURPOSE

God is my priority, and my job as a mother is my second priority. I know people may wonder where my husband fits into my priorities, but we are one. We agree that God is first, and our child is second. I was telling my friend about the progress of my son. He has grown immensely recently, as seen in even small things. For example, he used to be nervous about ordering or asking for ketchup when we eat at restaurants. But with practice, he is now fearless in those social situations. I challenge him to articulate his goals and business ideas and I support him in accomplishing them. He knows at this point that he will not work for anyone. He will own his own business, travel, and live a fulfilling life.

When the fear that besets us all comes up, retrain your brain to look for the solutions to the task at hand. Remove the barriers you see and let go of the obstacles tied to fear, shame, or your past. My Awakening Birthday removed my fear, shame, and the limits of my past. I am ready now to speak clearly. I attended a coaching session where I was asked to name something I was afraid of, and I could think of nothing.

That is where this book begins. My Awakening Birthday was not only about taking my medicine and watching what I eat. It was also about pulling back the curtain on the trauma that supported (or supports) fear, shame, and limitations. I am now fearless to face all three, and I have woken up to my purpose and progress in addressing these things. I share this because I believe my experience can be inspirational for others. Take care of the basics, then work through the trauma and experience resurrection just as I did.

CHAPTER 2
Mother's Message

Most of what I learned from my mother was how to "learn as you go." She gave birth to me when she was twenty-two years old, and I am the oldest of her three girls. I have two sisters through my mother—Latrisha and Tina—and to this day, my mother insists that she was "way too loose" in parenting us. She thinks she was looser on the reins with her children in response to how she was parented. My mother told me that Ganny (my grandmother) was stringent. What Ganny taught my mother was one part of her upbringing, and my mother's search for love consumed the other. Consequently, while my mother was going through her own growth experiences, she would teach us life lessons, but she was more focused on our growth rather than monitoring our every action.

MY MOTHER'S TRAUMA PRODUCED SIMPLICITY

My biological father, Robert, and my mother, Laquita, got married in 1982. They met at a skating rink when my mother was nineteen years old. My mother was young, and she allowed the relationship to deepen quickly. I thought that the two of them had so much affection toward one another—going out for dinner dates and other romantic stuff that couples do—but that never happened. They dated for six months before they got married. Mom was going to college, but she was having hard times and getting bad grades. He wanted to get married, and she felt that was a good way for her to get out of going to college.

My parents were not married because they were in love. My mother filed for divorce because my father was physically abusive. One day, she couldn't put up with the abuse anymore. I am sure my mother and father were happy for a time. Though their marriage ended within only a few years, at least they attempted to make it work. My mother stated that being married was different for her because she was raised by her mother and did not learn how a wife and husband were meant to be in love and be happy. Her father was not present during her childhood.

When I was three years old, I witnessed my parents getting divorced because of domestic violence. My children and grandchildren will never have to go through anything like that. I have learned that children often emulate the good and bad things they see modeled by their parents or whoever raised them. My father certainly did. I know that my grandparents love my father and his siblings, after all, they gave life to them. Sometimes, love is expressed and expected in different ways.

I attended church and was taught different love. I learned that God (our heavenly parent) loves us so much that He sent His only Son to die for our sins so that we may have eternal life and that nothing can separate us from God's love, not even our fears, challenges, and sins.

1 Corinthians 13:4-8 (NIV): "Love is patient, love is kind. It does not envy, it does not boast, it is not proud. It does not dishonor others, it is not self-seeking, it is not easily angered, it keeps no record of wrongs. Love does not delight in evil but rejoices with the truth. It always protects, always trusts, always hopes, always perseveres. Love never fails. But where there are prophecies, they will cease; where there are tongues, they will be stilled; where there is knowledge, it will pass away."

However, despite this parental love, my father learned some terrible things in his childhood that he brought into his own family. Sometimes, I imagined how tough it was for my father as a child to witness his father abuse his mother. My paternal grandparents celebrated their sixtieth anniversary together before my grandfather passed. Even though there was domestic violence and drug use, they were able to maintain a relationship for six decades.

I was a girl who grew up watching her parents get separated when she was just three. I believed that men dominate relationships and that women can only try to put up with them or submit to them. That's what I believed the world was like. What I learned about love, responsibility, and family relationships was totally different. My mother was likewise the product of a home without a stable family pattern. Her mother was their family's sole supporter, parent, and breadwinner. Her father simply wasn't around. My mother remembers that he left home when she was just a few years old. She didn't see him again until she was thirty-five.

My biological father had his own home business fixing vehicles, and he was in and out of prison. I have one memory of my father pushing my mother down a hill, but I was too young at that time to make anything out of what I witnessed. Just to be clear, he was not a terrible man. As a young child, I learned how to love loud music. My father loves loud music and he taught me how to sleep with it on. He also enjoyed rough-and-tumble play. He fed me and he enjoyed teaching us how to fix things.

My father also cheated constantly. I was told that he once chased down and beat my stepmother because she walked in on him cheating with another woman; he always had multiple girlfriends. My father used violence as a means of power and control. My mother endured the experience because she loved him, and she did not have a better example of what a man should be. She was fun-loving and accepting. He was fun as well, but with a dangerous temper and a need for control.

When my mom left my biological father, we moved into a shelter. My grandmother didn't want the baby to go to the shelter; she wasn't old enough to walk. My grandmother agreed with my mother to raise her and took in my younger sister, Tina. My grandmother raised my sister with care but was very specific about who she could spend time with. Even after my mom got a safe place to live, my younger sister remained with my grandmother. Tina was fourteen before she returned to my mother's house as she just wanted to live with her sisters. Just as most teens do, we argued often but we all knew that we loved each other. Before Tina got her own bed, she would sneak to get in my bed with me at night.

My mother is the oldest of her siblings. She and her siblings were conceived by a father who was always flittering, in and outside of the house. He was not a stable influence in her life, and as a result, my grandmother could not train her on what she did not know; she could not teach her what a man should be. Consequently, my mother could not teach me what a man should be.

My mother's father is still the same. He is still alive and, ironically, lives next door to my mother. He's been there for years and seems to care nothing about getting to know his children, grandchildren, or great-grandchildren. It's crazy to me! It does not bother my mother. She has told me that she has forgiven him.

Due to watching television shows as I grew up, I thought that the family was meant to operate within strict traditional roles. I was taught that the father should be a hardworking and stern breadwinner, while the mother should be a supporter and a hard worker around the home. This perspective would prove fatally one-dimensional in my adult relationships, but it was simple for my mother.

That simplicity is a blessing and a curse that I have worked to deconstruct for my own life and relationships. For example, one of my uncles was convicted, sentenced to more than six decades, and incarcerated for systematically and repeatedly raping his stepchildren. I love my uncle, but I feel that what he did to my cousins is horrible and unforgivable. I remember that my mom once wanted to see him. I could not understand why she would want to see a person who did such despicable things, so I asked her why. My mom responded, "Well, God has forgiven him, so we are going to forgive him."

I wanted to make sure that when my mother went to see her brother in prison, I went as well. I felt so angry and disgusted thinking about him the whole way there. I felt the same way when he walked to our table. When I saw him, I remember wishing he would go away. I didn't even want to see him. Within about fifteen minutes of my mom talking with him, I had a different thought: *That is my uncle! I love him!*

With that thought came memories: I used to run to give him hugs when I saw him. I remember that he used to have a lot of animals, and I once picked up one of his snakes and got bitten. I was not afraid of animals because I used to be around them at his house. After seeing him in prison, I felt so confused because I knew what he did to my cousins and couldn't come to terms with how I was supposed to keep loving him. I cried for hours. (My uncle is supposed to get out of prison in the year 2091. That should tell you what terrible things he did to my cousins.)

I remember that when things troubled me, my mother would always say, "Pray to God." She would not have anything more to add or talk about. Life is simple for her; she allows things to happen independently as the days go by. Plans are made, forgotten, or followed up on, but life goes on simply. I decided several years ago not to worry about the processing, mental status, or diagnoses of others. I used to argue about things, but I refuse to allow others' perspectives to bother me anymore. I had to learn about forgiveness. I accept the simplicity that my mother enjoys. I have chosen simplicity in my relationship with her.

EVERYONE IS DIFFERENT

My mother tried her best to give me the best life possible. She took care of my education and everything else around the home. From grades six through eight, I went to Hoover Middle School, a school with predominately African American students. For high school, I went to Northeast Academy. Through it all, my mom and my great aunt, Wanda, taught me the importance of education and I took those lessons to heart.

I did well in school and always earned acceptable grades. My mother was my constant support, even though she was not always very vocal or engaged (largely on account of her having to work a lot). A great example of this was when I had to apply for high school. My cousin took me to drop off the application. She was in the eleventh grade; I was in eighth grade. I did not talk to my mom about applying, I just did it. I think it is cool that I applied for school rather than skipping school on the Friday before spring break like many of my classmates. When the time came to decide about higher education, it seemed normal for me to go to college. After my baccalaureate degree, I did not discuss obtaining my master's degree with my mother either, I just applied.

The relationship I have with my son is different from my relationship with my mother. I spent much more time with him than my mother did with me because she had to work a lot. My goal is to provide the best environment for his growth, together with my husband. My son will often tell me random stories and report on the day; I never did that as a child. I talked with cousins or friends at school, but I did not talk with my mom. Because of our strong relationship, I have never felt like I missed out on anything going on in my son's life.

Everyone has a different childhood. Even my husband's story of coming from a great, intact family is not perfect. I don't feel like anyone can compare stories. Our experiences are just different.

RESILIENCY

Once I finished my baccalaureate degree, it was a chance encounter with a friend that got me interested in counseling. I have been told that I am incredibly empathetic and one of the best listeners and supporters a person could ask for. These are the skills I bring to the counseling profession. Maybe my experience with my mother and father taught me that you cannot always fix things; sometimes, you just have to listen. The lessons I have learned, I have lived. Though I brought my own gifts to the profession, I have also learned a tremendous amount from my training. Though tempted, I have chosen to refrain from doing any work to diagnose relatives or ruminate about my experiences growing up. (I have thought about my father's dysfunction, but not to the point of diagnosis. He fascinates me though. He would make a great case study.)

I avoided doing so because experts conclude that it is not always a good idea. It can be exhausting, and there's a clear danger of bias and overall lack of objectivity. It is also important to maintain boundaries. While I was working on my master's degree, I did venture to do some work on myself in relation to my past, but I never gave myself a diagnosis. I do remember that—perhaps this should be obvious—my father and stepfather brought up heavy emotions.

I just accept that the past is the past. Often, parents don't know better, and I want those whom I influence to remain open to learning. Just because you have children does not mean you know how to be the best parent. If you remain open, you will not shut down the opportunity to read, watch, and listen to positive or moral information about parenting or other subjects.

When I was five years old, my mother married another man. I never hesitated once when calling him Daddy, as I was convinced that he was indeed the best guy I had ever met. He acted like a father figure. Again, as a five-year-old child, I did not see anything sinister in my environment or the people around me. That marriage ended in divorce, and they separated when I was thirteen.

My mom's current husband, her third, is a wonderful person. They married when I was twenty-three, and at the time of this writing, they have been together for over twelve years. He is a deacon in the church, a good husband, and a wonderful life companion. Unlike my mother's last two husbands, I honestly think he's a great man. I know he will not let the family down.

MY MOM'S MESSAGE

"Don't let how you were raised dictate how you want to live your life. Some children are raised with alcoholic parents, but they refuse to become alcoholics themselves. You may have been raised in an abusive home, but you have decided, 'The abuse stops with me. I won't let my children go through what I went through.' Parents desire that their children have opportunities they didn't have and that they succeed in life and have more than they did. I was raised on welfare and food stamps, and I decided that would not be how I raised my children, so I worked hard. It is up to you to break the cycle and take a different path. A path that you have chosen because the sky is the limit." — Laquita

CHAPTER 3

The Complexity of Men

MY FIRST FATHER FIGURE

My stepfather was the first man I really knew because my mother divorced my biological father when I was three years old. I would see my biological father once or twice a month when he wasn't in jail. He was not a consistent father, so my stepfather filled that role.

He worked during the day and would spend time with my sisters and me in the evening. That's when my mother would go to work. For the first nine years of our relationship, everything was fun and safe. We would hang out, watch movies, and chill. Every summer, we would travel, and my stepfather would bring his biological son with us for vacations and weekends. Anytime school was out, my stepfather was there with us. We called him Daddy and contentedly lived with him as an example of a father in the home. I was too young to think anything different. I did not question anything. I considered him to be a good man even though, as a child, I had no one to compare him to and no objective way to evaluate him.

When I was twelve years old, something changed. I found out later that he had a crack cocaine addiction. Though I didn't know what was going on at the time, I've reflected on it seriously at various points in my adult life.

I was about to enter my teen years and I started going through puberty. Among other physical changes, my breasts were developing, making me a young woman. With my parents working different shifts, my mother was rarely home when my stepfather was. At times, when she wasn't home, he would have me rub his back under the pretense that he was teaching me how to give massages. He had a history of back pain, so I thought it made sense that he would need a back massage. He would also rub my back in return, telling me it was so I would know how good the massage felt. I'm not sure when those situations first shifted from massage training to molestation, but all I can remember is him telling me to turn over and remove my bra in the middle of a massage. He started to rub my breasts.

My mother was so busy with her work that, at first, she failed to notice the negative changes happening in her husband and his addiction. But over the next few months, they began to argue more frequently. That's when my mom started to notice the change in him. My stepfather also became very abusive, and our home became a place of domestic violence. At that point, I was sure that he was not the father I once thought he was.

One summer day, when I was thirteen, my mom decided to escape with my younger sister and me. She felt that our home was no longer a safe environment. We drove for a while just to get out of the house, but we ended up returning to the house because my mother felt we had nowhere else to go. We entered the house, and my mother and stepfather began to argue. The argument spiraled out of control. I noticed that there was a gun on top of the microwave. When my stepfather picked it up, my sister started screaming at the top of her lungs. I picked up the phone and called 911. The police showed up and arrested him. That night, I knew that my mom's second marriage was about to end. Sure enough, my parents separated and that was the end of their marriage of ten years.

That experience, combined with my stepfather molesting me, left me confused because he was a good man in the beginning. How could he have changed? I concluded that I could not trust men and matter-of-factly added to my Life Lessons List: *do not trust men.*

MY BIOLOGICAL FATHER

With my family split, we were forced to live with different people during that time of turmoil. My mother was in one place, I was in another place, and each of my sisters were also living in different places. While we were grateful to relatives for taking us in, it was difficult to be apart.

My biological father remained in touch during that time, though we never spent much time with him. When we did see him, he would pick my sisters and me up and drop us off at our stepmother's house. (After his relationship with my mother, my biological father remarried. Together, he and his wife had a couple of children.) Their household provided me with three additional sisters. I had a great time with all of them. My biological father also continued to be a womanizer. My sisters told me about that. He would stay gone for days on end.

I never thought of him as a good man. He was in and out of jail, inconsistent, and unreliable. As my sisters and I got older, he would tell us to pack up our stuff for a weekend visit, then not show up. It took me a while to understand the type of man he was. One of my sisters and I would argue about him sometimes. I told her that I was not going to prepare for visits from him. I would wait until he showed up before packing because him showing up was not a given.

The lessons I learned from my biological father were not always positive because his example was not a good one. He was consistent in one thing though: to this day, he is the same person he has always been. He is a drinker, untrustworthy, and abusive... consistently. This isn't to say that he is 100 percent evil, of course. I remember many times when he made my sisters and I laugh and although he often stood us up, we did have some good times together. There was even a time when he sacrificed for me. He gave me a 1979 Monte Carlo car when I was sixteen years old. Perhaps, for that reason, as I continued my life through school, my career, and marriage, I never ascribed negatives to him. He just is who he is, and I have accepted him for that reality.

TRIED TO GET "LOVE"

When I was twelve years old, in the seventh grade, and in middle school, I had a boyfriend named Joseph who lived near us. We used to ride the same bus to school. I used to spend time with him at his house to watch movies. One day, he told me to meet him at a friend's house. I went there to keep him happy, as I was trying to get love. After that, I was no longer a virgin, and my boyfriend did not love me as I expected.

When I was fourteen years old, I worked a job with my father's friend during the summer. He owned a BBQ restaurant, and I was hired to help clean and take orders. I also got signed up for a summer reading program, and I got paid for that too!

At that time, I met a guy named Floyd. He was a year older than me, and we were both in summer school. Our jobs were close in proximity. We spent a lot of time together during the summer. My ususal routine was to ride the bus to the summer reading class then ride the bus to work at the BBQ place.

One day, while I was on my way to work, Floyd and I walked around the street and ended up at his house. We began kissing, and we had sex. In hindsight, I understand that I was just attempting to find love, but I didn't know how to get it. All I wanted was for someone to take notice of me and treat me sweetly.

Because of our sexual activities, I got to work very late, and my father was looking for me. He took me to his house and whooped me with a belt. He whooped me so much that my bottom was hard, red, purple, and black from bruises. For days it hurt to sit down, and that night I dreamt that I stabbed him to death!

My many relationships with men over the years taught me to look out for being used. It took me a while to realize that to satisfy my desire for loving treatment, I would allow men to offer pretend sweetness so that they could get sex in return.

That was exemplified by how one boy treated me in junior high school. He would always ask for hugs when I wore tight-fitting clothes. He was not as interested in hugs when I wore loose-fitting clothing. At the time, my breasts were getting more significant. I later realized that he only wanted the hugs to feel my breasts against his chest, and I was okay with that because I valued the positive attention. One day, he came in for a hug and noticed my hairy armpit. (My mother never told me that I should keep that area manicured.) That boy broadcasted it to everyone around by shouting, "Damn! Look at your hairy armpits."

I knew at that moment that what I thought was positive attention or a mutual interaction was only him using me for his benefit. He did not care about me, and I added that to my list: "Oh, here is another man that cannot give me what I need."

I have learned that a father sets the standard, but I did not have any man to set the standard. I have learned the standard from my father-in-law. I learned that the father should spend time with his child, provide positive guidance and discipline, be a good role model, teach the child about right and wrong, and respect the mother.

Since both my husband and I have learned this standard, we are not harsh on our son, and we make sure that we are not too busy for him. I learned that since my father never told me how beautiful I was, I sought for other men to tell me. I went out and tried to fill that void with someone else. To be clear, I did feel love from my mother; Ganny; my great aunt; and my great-grandmother, Granny. But despite the love those women showered on me, I still craved love from men—most notably from the good father figure I never had.

My husband and I set a high standard. That will be our legacy. That is what we are passing down, more than our money, our success, or our accomplishments. Our values and what we believe in are what we're going to live on. We decided to model excellence and integrity. We will give our son the blessing, let him know that he was made in God's image, and tell him that he is extremely valuable and has seeds of greatness on the inside. If you have children, there is a void that you can fill as their father. You can set a high standard. That will be your legacy.

For the many single mothers doing an incredible job raising their children without the help of a man, God said He will be your help. He will help you raise your child, give you wisdom, and provide for your needs. God will be your help and take care of you and your children.

It's never too late to bless your children. Your parents may not have done this. You may not have been raised this way, but you can pick up the phone and call your son or daughter. They may be fully grown, and you may not have spoken to them in a while, but you can call and tell your daughter how proud you are and how much you love her, or you can tell your son you think he is amazing. Your approval, even later in life, can be a turning point for them.

FORGIVENESS

Growing up, many things made me angry, stressed, and hateful such as domestic violence, child molestation, and poverty. As an adult, I could add on depression, infidelity, and trauma. Christian forgiveness is a very topical issue today for several reasons. Forgiveness is a choice. And since God commands us to forgive, we must make a conscious choice to obey Him and ignore the hurt in our lives. Hurt people hurt people. The perpetrator may not want forgiveness and may never change, but their choice doesn't negate God's desire for us to have a forgiving spirit. Ideally, the perpetrator will seek redress. But if not, the victim can still decide to forgive them.

Of course, it is impossible to entirely forget about the pain inflicted upon us through the sinful acts of others or ourselves. We cannot selectively erase those events from our memory. But the Bible says that God will never remember our sins again. God knows we "have all sinned and do not obtain the glory of God" (Romans 3:23, NIV). But since we have been forgiven through Christ, we are justified in our standing (or in court). Heaven is ours as if our sins never happened. If we belong to Him through our faith in Christ, God does not condemn us for our sins. Whether we choose to agree with each other or not, forgiveness is critical in our relationships.

The decision to forgive is usually conscious and intentional. That does not mean that the perpetrator deserves your forgiveness or even that they asked for it. Forgiveness is something you do for yourself.

As Marianne Williamson said, "Unforgiveness is like drinking poison yourself and waiting for the other person to die." That would never happen! Forgiveness helps to remove the block of corrosive anger and gives you peace of mind. It is choosing to shield your heart from thoughts of hatred. Most of all, forgiveness is you letting go of the baggage of anger, malice, grudges, hurt, pain, and betrayal, and surrendering it all to God. In this sense, God "forgives and forgets."

In 1 Corinthians 13:4-6, the Bible shows us that unselfish love is the very foundation for true forgiveness because Godly love "does not keep account of evil."

It is worth mentioning again that forgiveness is not a feeling but a choice. And since the flesh is unwilling to yield to anything that helps us become more Godlike, choosing the path of forgiveness means that you need to ask God for the power to forgive.

God's ability to forgive is at work in every one of His children, and once the choice to forgive is made, God makes help available. Whatever has happened to you, know this: it is possible to practice God's way of forgiveness!

These three steps are essential to forgiving someone or cultivating a heart of forgiveness:

1. **Surrender to God:** Forgiveness is about surrendering to the will of the Father, letting go of baggage, and unclogging the connection that exists between you and Him. You need to give time to the study of the Scriptures and meditate on their meaning. The strength to forgive comes from God. Let prayer guide your daily living as you follow His will. Here is an example of a simple daily prayer to cultivate a heart that forgives: "Master, help me not to be insulted today. Keep me from pointless outrage. If I am angry at somebody, show me what the root is. Give me the strength to pardon that person."

2. **Decide to forgive:** As much as forgiveness is not just an act, you still need to make the deliberate decision to remember that God provides the help and you put in the effort. This decision does not mean you overlook the wrong that was done or gloss over the fact that it happened. Remember that you are letting it go instead of holding on and that you are allowing yourself to heal. Sometimes

saying, "I forgive so-and-so" might be a part of it, but it is more than that. Regardless of how painful the decision to forgive is, it is worth it. As you walk more on the path of forgiveness, you will discover that forgiveness is a matter of the earlier done the better. It is better to forgive as soon as you can rather than let your anger fester.

3. **Remember that to err is human:** You need to understand that forgiveness is risky, as human beings will always fail you. Everyone is imperfect, and a forgiven offender still has the probability of offending again, even if he was sorry the first time. It is just human nature, and you, as a believer, must realize that. If the very beginning of our relationship with God was based on forgiveness, we should appreciate that and forgive the mistakes of others too. This might look like a hard thing to do but remember the commandment of Jesus in Matthew 5:44 (KJV): "But I say unto you, love your enemies, bless them that curse you, do good to them that hate you, and pray for them which despitefully use you, and persecute you." In a book by Charles Capps he said, "Unforgiveness will stop your faith from

working." He also stated, "Your faith will fail to produce if you live in strife or unforgiveness. You have opened the door to Satan. You have invited him in, and he will show up every time. Tragedy has come to Christian homes because of unforgiveness."

Finally, the utmost beneficiary from an act of forgiveness is you. You cannot afford to keep hurt and anger locked up inside of you. Unforgiveness is a destroyer. God's way is the way of forgiveness, and God's love is a forgiving one. God has pardoned you, now the time has come for you to do the same with others. Decide to forgive today and receive the Lord's help.

"To forgive is to set a prisoner free and discover that person was you."
—Lewis B. Smedes

CHRISTIANS SEEK TO PLEASE GOD, NOT MAN

I have known for a long time that we are supposed to love others, but I have slowly learned over the years that loving others does not always mean that you need to please them. While we need to love our fellow man, we should be more concerned about pleasing God.

The apostle Paul wrote in a letter to the members of the churches in Galatia, "Am I now trying to win the approval of human beings, or God? Or am I trying to please people? If I were still trying to please people, I would not be Christ's servant" (Galatians 1:10, God's Word).

The words of the last line are very powerful: "If I were still trying to please people, I would not be Christ's servant." These words are more suitable now than ever before, even though they were written almost two thousand years ago.

Under the act of love for people, the spirit of human suitability has penetrated the Church. This spirit encourages people to seek love from people, not from God. The principle "love your neighbor" is replaced by the principle "do not displease your neighbor," and instead of discovering the truth, there is only hypocrisy to be found.

What Happens to a Person When He Begins to Please People, Not God?

Such a believer begins to rely on people and seek their favor. And whether it happens sooner or later, a man-pleaser will inevitably become a hypocrite. He will compromise with sin because he wants to please a person, just like I did when I had sex at the age of twelve to please a boy.

As time passes, the man-pleaser will begin to persecute everything that disturbs their peace. They will persecute God's prophets and even reject His Word when it is not compatible with the principle "do not displease your neighbor."

Why are Those Who Seek to Please People Not Afraid to Do Evil?

Many who do evil in the name of pleasing their fellow man are not afraid of doing evil because they hope that by pleasing others, they will be saved from the responsibility of their actions. This is exactly how fascist soldiers justified themselves when they said, "We only carried out the order."

Those who seek to please their fellow man are not concerned with whether they are doing the right thing as much as they are concerned about whether everyone is happy with them or not. The main thing for them is not what they do, but who they please with their actions. And when they realize that they have pleased someone, they experience a false sense of innocence.

The spirit of seeking to please man often gives rise to an uncritical attitude towards sin, and at the same time, rejection of those who rebel against sin.

We need to be aware of Satan's tactic to deceive us and tempt us into evil. We cannot let our efforts to love our fellow man become twisted and lead us to seek to please man more than God, for pleasing God before all else is the only way to experience true joy and happiness in our lives. We should help people but not at the expense of neglecting ourselves and being unfulfilled, overwhelmed, and resentful because we are not comfortable with saying no.

CHAPTER 4
Self-Esteem and Friendship

I have had many best friends throughout my life, starting in elementary school and progressing onward through adulthood. At various times, I thought many of these people and I were best friends forever (BFFs). Sadly, I was wrong more often than I was right.

Whenever one of these friends stopped being friendly or I felt rejected, it would really get to me. I would think about and stress over what I did, what they did, whether the relationship could be fixed or not, whether it mattered if they were in my life or not, and many other anxiety-fueled questions. I have lost multiple friends for various reasons, which was always confusing to me because I always tried to be a good friend. Every time one of my friends walked away, the feeling that I was not worthy grew inside of me.

I was such a people pleaser growing up, constantly seeking validation, acceptance, and appreciation. I always wanted to make sure I never made my friends upset. I never messed up on purpose. I would do anything just to show them how much I cared about them. Having friendships was always important to me (sometimes too important) and a massive source of my self-esteem.

Self-esteem comes from having a strong belief in who you are and what you can do. Naturally, believing in your ability to do something—make friends, for example—then accomplishing that goal results in increased feelings of self-esteem. But there are several attributes you need to obtain before you can build true self-esteem, such as self-awareness, self-trust, and self-care. Failure to obtain these attributes before seeking self-esteem can lead you to question your self-worth and your abilities when things don't go your way or you fail to reach certain goals that matter to you.

Low self-esteem may stem from experiences in early childhood. If you did not fit in at school, had difficulty meeting your parents' expectations, or were neglected or abused, you may have unknowingly adopted negative core beliefs about yourself. These deeply ingrained beliefs often go unnoticed but are extremely powerful.

Teenagers, especially young girls, may be subject to unhelpful messages and ideals on social media and in the media generally that lead them to believe that their worth is based on how they look or behave. This belief may lead to low self-esteem and negative thoughts about their self-worth. Performing poorly at school or being bullied can also cause low self-esteem for years. Stressful life events, such as an unhappy relationship, bereavement, or serious illness may also cause low self-esteem.

If we do not do the emotional work on ourselves that we need to do, our self-esteem will rise and fall with every change that happens in our lives. Living with fluctuating self-worth is exhausting and unsustainable. You do not want to feel good about who you are every time you make a friend then feel bad about who you are every time one walks out of your life. The same goes for any other circumstance. You do not want how you feel about yourself to move like a roller coaster based on what job you have, your current weight, or your relationship status.

Over the last few years, I have lost more close friends. But it didn't stress me out or threaten to topple my self-esteem like it did for most of my life. I did deep work on myself and have finally learned lessons that help keep my self-esteem high and stable.

The lessons I learned were hard for me to see when I was caught up in them; they are the kind that only hindsight makes clear. But as time passed, I learned that losing friendships is just a part of growing up. I never really wanted that statement to be true, but over the last few years, I have become more comfortable with that idea. I do not need a lot of friends to be happy; I'll take quality over quantity any day. I also learned that I can't force friendships; both people need to contribute to the relationship. Balanced friendships are my jam now, and I would not have it any other way. I do not regret the past friendships that were lopsided. They have taught me so much, and for that I am incredibly grateful.

If you are currently going through a bit of a friendship breakup yourself, here are some tips that have helped me along the way:

1. **Sit with it.** These are your feelings, and you are entitled to them. They are valid, you are valid, and so are all of your concerns. Sit with your feelings and acknowledge them. Give them a name, hold space for them, and do not judge them. Know that what you're going

through is temporary. Feelings are not facts, remember that.

2. **Write it out.** If just sitting with your feelings is not doing enough for you, try writing them out. You might not even be fully aware of what you are writing once you get started but keep writing down your feelings until you begin to feel a release. Acknowledge your part in the friendship, make note of lessons you have learned, and notice where you can improve as a person.

3. **Have a chat.** Talk out your feelings with another good friend, a family member, a life coach, or a therapist. Expressing yourself and embracing vulnerability by talking it out with someone will cause great shifts in your life and in your perspective. You can even ask friends for constructive criticism if that is what you want. You can ask questions about how you excel as a friend, what might need work, and how you can improve the relationships that are currently important in your life. NOTE: I recommend not involving friends who are within the same friend group as the person who is leaving your life. There

is no need to alter someone else's feelings or try to manipulate the situation in your favor.

4. **Be brave and trust that you are going to be okay.** This is tough, and I get it. Be patient, be kind, and be gentle with yourself. It's normal for this process to be difficult. A great question I tend to ask myself is, "Will this matter in a year or five years?" Most of the time, the answer is a solid "no." Take the time you need to feel free from the situation and have confidence in knowing this is all a part of your personal growth.

5. **Express gratitude.** Gratitude is incredibly powerful, and I encourage you to acknowledge all you already have going for you. Be grateful for the memories you had and for the guidance this friendship brought you over time. Even though the relationship is over now, it's okay to remember fond memories and moments that make you laugh or smile. You do not have to hate the person either. You can respect them, be grateful for the times you had together, and gently move on. Forgiving that person and yourself is key. Gratitude will help you forgive. Also,

share your gratitude with the friends you have now. Call them up and tell them why you love them and what you're most thankful for about them. Notice the qualities in those friendships that are working well and how those qualities and core values are in line with yours. It helps to know what is most important to you in a relationship and to stick to your boundaries moving forward.

Friendship break-ups aren't easy, but I know you'll get through this. Persevere, accept, forgive, and you'll become a better person. Throughout it all, never question your self-worth. Friendships come and go, but your worth is infinite.

How do you have confidence when you do not have any friends? The secret I've learned is to shift your focus away from your lack of friends and focus on the positive things in your life that make you happy or provide some level of fulfillment. Stop being afraid of having no friends and see the experience as an opportunity to grow and ultimately become a person who attracts the kinds of friends you want.

MAKING FRIENDS IN ADULTHOOD

Although you shouldn't ever be frightened by the thought of losing friends, friendships can bring fulfillment and support into your life. Having a BFF, even if it doesn't truly last forever, can be a wonderful thing. One of the best things about having good friends is that they can strengthen you and your faith. They can make you a better person.

At one time in my life, I did everything I could to make sure that I had my husband and my BFF. I wanted these roles to be filled by two different people. I wanted someone separate to complain about my husband to. I wanted someone I could spill the drama, gossip, and share complaints with that I couldn't tell my husband. I have since realized that for me, my husband is my BFF. Since I have grown, I see now that I can be open with my husband. Like a true BFF should, my husband has changed my life and inspired me to be better. He is an amazing example of faith and devotion! I believe your spouse should always be your true BFF. After all, ideally, they will stay with you your whole life while other friendships will fade with time.

But that doesn't mean you can't have wonderful friendships! I know that you just need a friend to talk to sometimes. I also know that making friends as an adult is different than making friends as a child and, in many ways, it's harder. Here are a few suggestions for finding and making friends that I have found useful.

1. **Make a wish list of your ideal BFFs.** Think of people you've met who you'd like to get to know better. If no one comes to mind, list some traits that you would like your new BFF to have. This will help you recognize the people with whom you should invest time building a relationship.

2. **List qualities you'd like to see more of in yourself.** Closely related to the last suggestion, think about the type of person you want to be and consider who can bring those traits out of you. The more you know yourself and what you're looking for, the better off you'll be and the less time you'll waste. Listing qualities that you'd like to see more of in yourself (or that you like about yourself and want to have amplified) can attract people who bring out your best self over the long run. Keep in mind that the traits you'd like to be brought out in you by your BFF (and those you'd like

them to have) can be different from the traits you'd expect from a spouse or partner.

3. **Join a new club or organization.** It's easier to get to know people when you regularly spend time with them. Get involved in an activity that matters to you where you're likely to meet others with similar values and interests. You'll automatically have something to connect over, and some of these relationships might become long-lasting friendships with time.

4. **Take initiative.** If you want to get to know someone better, you don't need to wait for them to reach out to you or otherwise make the first move. Instead, become a kind initiator, even if you're an introvert. Most people like to make friends, and some may be looking for a BFF just like you. Strike up a conversation and share something about yourself. Ask them to share about themselves. Small talk is fine in the first interaction. Your goal is to break the ice and look for shared interests.

5. **Stay in touch and follow up.** Once you have interacted with a person and exchanged contact information, don't forget to call or

message them. Many relationships get off to a great start but end in, "We should hang out sometime." If you had a good connection, reach out and continue the relationship. Call them and invite them to meet up or just talk on the phone. Opening up to someone frequently is a great way to develop a strong friendship. Just make sure the interest is mutual so it doesn't bother the other person.

6. **Be consistent.** Be on time when you make plans with someone. Do not text them twenty minutes before and say you'll be twenty minutes late, or worse, cancel at the last minute. Small things like being on time build trust in any relationship.

7. **Say yes.** You might have to go outside of your comfort zone and try new things to make new connections. The key is to be willing to put yourself out there to engage with people you don't know well (or at all). Of course, this can be intimidating, especially for people who are shy or who experience social anxiety. But taking the risk to meet new people is what leads to the reward of developing new relationships. As much as your inner social

butterfly allows, say "yes" when you receive invitations from others. You never know how fun it will be until you try it. And the more you put yourself out there, the more people you'll meet. Letting friends and family know you want to make new friends can help as well. They can introduce you to people and invite you along to events and activities.

8. **Focus on bonding with like-minded people.** You'll likely find it easier to bond with people who have goals that are similar to yours, which is great. But like-minded also encompasses opinions and interests. Finding people you can learn and grow with is the name of the game. This applies to your faith as well. 1 Thessalonians 5:11 teaches us to "encourage one other and build each other up." The phrase "build each other up" is regularly used to describe the work of believers in relationships. We can build our brothers and sisters up in many ways, including through prayer, encouragement, and fellowship in worship. "Building up" can mean promoting a friend's growth or helping them to stand strong.

9. **Focus on quality not quantity.** Working to build a relationship with someone you really connect with will be the best-case scenario in the long run. To be honest, it's exhausting to commit yourself to hanging out with a million different people. So, focus on the people with whom you truly want to build deeper relationships.

10. **Know when to let go.** We aren't meant to hold on to every single connection we make. It is important to deepen meaningful relationships, but it's also okay to drift away from some people. Whether we're moving, growing up, or changing, sometimes we lose certain connections—and that is okay! The more we can do to normalize and allow for that kind of change, the better we will be at shifting our attention to the relationships and friendships that we really need and value.

11. **Be conscious of how you present yourself.** This may seem obvious, but if you smell, are dirty, or tend to present yourself in a sloppy way, you may turn some potential friends off. We all have off days (it happens!) but

presenting yourself with care shows that you value yourself.

12. **Befriend good people who build you up.** Paul tells us that "evil company corrupts good habits." 2 Corinthians 6:14 (NIV) reads: "Do not be yoked together with unbelievers. For what do righteousness and wickedness have in common? Or what fellowship can light have with darkness?" In Galatians 5:22-23 (NIV), Paul lists nine characteristics of the fruit of the Spirit: love, joy, peace, longsuffering, kindness, goodness, faithfulness, gentleness, and self-control. How much would each of these characteristics do for friendships? He continues: "Let us not become conceited, provoking one another, envying one another" (Galatians 5:26, NIV).

If we truly live as God teaches us in His instruction manual (the Bible), we will make more friends, and others will enjoy being in our company. We will also be better equipped to be a good friend, and we will put ourselves in a position to earn the respect of others who can also become our good friends!

13. Love yourself. It's so much easier to get other people to love you if you take the time to love yourself first. It's not as simple as it sounds, but it can help you make friends. You'll also find that when you love yourself, you'll feel better about yourself. This can make other challenges in your life easier to bear (though I'm not suggesting this is a cure for mental illness). To love yourself, try focusing on your physical health, making a list of small goals, or just doing something you enjoy every day. In the words of Reverend Ike Legacy, "It's not important what other people believe about you. It's only important what you believe about yourself."

CHAPTER 5

Relationship Day One

Life is a series of decisions. One of the biggest decisions we can make is how to pattern our lives. Based on what I understood about men, I was forced to develop a standard for evaluating them using only my (mostly poor) experiences as a guide. My mother could not tell me what standard I should have, as she herself didn't know, and my grandmother did not seem to know either, so I was left to create my own. When I met the man who would be my husband, my standard consisted of several traits:

1. A man must work.
2. A man should not put his hands on a woman violently for any reason.
3. A man must be trustworthy, whether he is being watched or not.
4. A man must be consistent and consistently good by making choices to move himself and his family forward.

5. A man must provide reciprocity—mutual benefit. We must both benefit from the relationship. It is not just about me taking care of his needs.

RICKEY

I have known Rickey for a very long time. We became friends when we were in elementary school. We were in the second grade together. I remember that he used to say he wanted to play on the school playground with me. Rickey would call me on the phone and often come to my grandmother's house and ask if I could come out and play. We were young, but I knew that he liked me. There was another boy who also liked me, and a girl in our class was always attempting to pit the two boys against each other for me.

I was too young to know what the words boyfriend and girlfriend meant. All I knew was that Rickey was sweet and fun to talk to.

I attended a different school for third grade, and Rickey and I did not talk again until we were in ninth grade. Our reunion occurred because I met a girl in high school with the same last name as him and remarked, "You look like my friend, Rickey, and you have the same last name." "That's my cousin!"

she responded. It turned out that Rickey's father and this girl's mother were siblings. I spoke with Rickey's cousin and got her to give me his phone number. I called him, and just like that, we were back. Rickey promptly asked me to be his girlfriend. It seemed like no time had passed, and before we knew it, we were talking on the phone almost every day.

After he graduated from high school, we decided to move in together. It was easy to make that decision because we got along very well. The pastor at my mother's church was passionate about not living together without being married. He taught us that living together without being married would send you directly to hell. I told Rickey that if we wanted to live together, we needed to get married. I don't remember Rickey's response; I just know that he did not fight the idea. I was nineteen when we got married. We were married in the pastor's office. It was just the pastor, a deacon, Rickey, and me. We did not tell anyone until after the ceremony. We didn't realize that our wedding announcement would be placed in the newspaper marriage announcements. That is how Rickey's family found out that we were married. After his family found out, we agreed to tell my family.

At the time, we had been together for five years. I remember one of my sisters, Tina, crying because I had eloped and didn't include her in the wedding. I remember some disparaging words being said, and an aunt told me, "You are going to be sad." I remember thinking, *Why would you say that?* The aunt who said that to me had been through a rough marriage, so I assumed that she didn't have anything good to say because of her negative experiences, and I didn't listen to her.

MARRIAGE WOES

After getting married to Rickey, I felt like I was dreaming; even though we were still young, my life was perfect. I felt joyful and safe with him. In college, I learned about children who were in foster care. I told Rickey that I would like to be a part of the solution, and he accepted the idea. I had a loving husband, and we decided to foster a child. We had a beautiful, small family and I loved the way things were going.

My thoughts about men were based primarily on the men I saw in my own life, and I was not about to take care of a man who was not working. Looking back, it was silly. Since I was fourteen, I had worked while Rickey had been involved in sports and other extracurricular activities. Once we were out of high school, his lifestyle became a problem for me. While I completed my advanced degree and found work, he spent his time hanging out with friends. I remember famously putting my foot down, telling him, "I am not about raising a grown man."

My husband was a former football player. He was massive (in a good way) and cut out for the sport. He would get jobs allowing him to use his physical strength, which typically lasted for several months. But eventually, the jobs would take a toll on his body, and he would end up out of work again. The arguments increased because I did not believe that he was trying. I felt like I had done the most to make ends meet, even lowering my standards in some ways. I felt like I was doing everything times three, and he was not doing much of anything to help support our family.

SEPARATION

I got hired at the Department of Human Services (DHS), and my head was filled with visions of handsome men with good jobs. I began to wonder why I was sticking with someone who was not putting forth a lot of effort, at least, not enough for me. Like every other marriage, Rickey and I also went through a rough patch.

We were in the same boat of impropriety—we were both lying to each other as we both cheated on each other multiple times. I know now how badly Rickey was looking for love and attention. He needed to feel unique and like he had worth, while I wanted someone in my life who was looking forward to something bigger. Someone with ambition.

We had two children at that time. Jaon and another foster child, James, who stayed with us for about two years (from age eight to ten) before he went to live with his grandmother. My husband took care of both boys, as he did not believe in daycare because he felt it wasn't safe. He is a great father, and I think that was why we stayed together for as long as we did, although it did not change my mindset towards him.

Jaon went to live with his biological mother for eighteen months (we later adopted him), while James was adopted by his grandmother, so we did not have the children staying with us and keeping us together. As a result, we decided to separate for a while. We never planned on filing for a divorce, but we decided it would be good to take a break and give each other some space to work out our differences.

We had been having issues with each other for about two years when we decided it was time to fix things, no matter the cost. In our situation, the cost was us living apart for three months straight. But the best part was that we found our way back to each other and are now living a happily married life.

Rickey's parents were married for twenty-five years so he knew, from their example, what it would take to have a happy marriage. I learned that most of what I knew about happy marriages was from college. We decided to take time to learn more about each other and show each other love. It took some time, especially since we were both still distanced and distracted, even during the periods when we would attend counseling.

With time and work, things got better. I remember going on dates again with Rickey during our period of separation. One time, he invited me over for dinner at his grandmother's house. He always dressed nicely when we spent time together, but that night he was incredibly dashing. After dinner, he presented me with a ring and asked if we could get back together. He never stopped loving me and wanting to be with me. He was genuinely trying. He enrolled in college and worked to get to a station in life that I could respect. He found his niche in entrepreneurship, and we could not be more satisfied together or individually.

I learned to communicate better. We can now discuss what I am feeling rather than me fussing. We learned how to explore solutions and listen to each other's point of view. Now, I understand more about him, his goals, and his aspirations. Now, I am a supporter, not a nag to him, while he is a foundation rather than a symbol for me. My marriage goal is the same as his, which allows us to bring out the best in each other.

My revised standards for a man are as follows:

1. He must be a protector. A man must take care of his wife and family.

2. He must live the king role. He must have a household plan, and he should share it with his wife.

3. He must be a communicator. No role is complete if it is not discussed with the family.

4. He must be a leader. A man must direct the household. In addition to having a plan, he must perfect the plan based on the family members' intimate knowledge and understanding.

My relationship with Rickey has matured over the years. I see his power, his skill, and his ability. When I had a ruptured brain aneurysm and I was in a coma, he took care of our son while helping to run my business, his business, our finances, our household, and other activities. But he would try to leave all of that behind to cry alone in our bed.

Rickey's sister, Ashley, and her son came quickly and were a great support to the family while I was in the hospital. She helped Rickey to calm down and de-stress, and her words helped his faith grow stronger. My sister, Latrisha, her husband, Kendall, and her kids came to stay at our house as well! They were there to support Rickey and Jaon daily. Kendall was a special help in the kitchen; he cooked most of the meals. Another person who came was my nephew, Jordan. He is about six months younger than Jaon, and they are like brothers.

Latrisha worked with me in my business, and she did so much to keep things running on that front. She took the initiative to keep track of important things, both in my business and my personal life. Rickey later showed me a note that Latrisha wrote. Her to-do list included figuring out payroll, going to the grocery store, determining questions to ask the doctor, and more!

I am so grateful for Latrisha, Ashley, and the others who pitched in to support my son, husband, and business when I needed them the most. With all of the family staying with us, our home became the true meaning of the saying, "It takes a village."

Many others showed up to help me and my family in other ways. Multiple friends and family were praying and fasting for me. But no one did more than my husband, Rickey. He was the superman of the story. Through it all, he showed himself to be my protector, king, communicator, and leader. "Wives, submit yourselves to your own husbands as you do to the Lord. For the husband is the head of the wife as Christ is the head of the church, his body, of which he is the Savior. Now as the church submits to Christ, so also wives should submit to their husbands in everything" (Ephesians 5:22-24, NIV). Since my Awakening Birthday, I have easily learned to submit to my husband.

CHAPTER 6

My Son the Blessing

The most important lesson I can teach my son is about love. I am teaching him how to both receive love and give love. The topic of love has been a difficult one for me because of how I was raised. I do not remember ever being taught about love. I rarely received hugs or kisses from my mother or father, and my stepfather's hugs and kisses started to become inappropriate over time.

My son has me, my husband, and my sisters to teach him what love is. Despite our upbringing, each of my sisters has learned to be caring and affectionate. We all decided to treat our children differently than we were treated growing up. This has changed our relationships with each other in that we are more supportive of each other than we were growing up and we have been able to develop true sisterly bonds.

God has entrusted my son to me and my husband. Jaon has a support system in my husband and me that will be his backbone his entire life. For me, the blessing is more than just his presence in my life;

he is my inspiration to step up to another level. I am not just responsible for taking him to school, but I am called to ensure that he is enrolled in a good school and gaining a good education. I know that God has a plan for his life, and as such, I am charged and empowered in the same way that John the Baptist's mother was charged and empowered. I have a son who will do great things, and my job is to ensure that he is prepared.

TEACH ME HOW TO LOVE

I learned about foster care when I was in college, and I was moved by the plight of children who had faced intense hardship at such tender ages and had consequently found themselves in need of a home.

Rickey and I wanted to open our home to a foster child, so we completed the required training in order to become foster parents. We finished on a Saturday and the next Monday they told us there was a baby who needed a place to stay. Jaon was our first foster child. He was born to a mother, Donna, who was in foster care herself, and she was only fifteen years old when she gave birth.

The foster parent experience was not always easy. When we first started fostering, Jaon was only six weeks old. When he was two years old, Donna was doing well, and she was in a foster home that was a safe place for Jaon to be placed. We tried to support her, but she did not allow us to see him. We were devastated and decided not to foster another child, so we closed our home. About a year later, she invited us to her high school graduation. They were living in a home that was about a two-hour drive away from us. We were very excited to see Jaon, but he didn't know who we were, and that was difficult for us.

When Jaon was three years old, the Department of Human Services worker called me to inquire whether we would open our home to foster Jaon again. She said that he could not stay at that home. When I told her "Yes," she immediately she asked, "Do you need to ask your husband?"

"Hell naw!" I replied. Rickey and I knew that we could not go through the heartache that would come with loving and losing another child in the foster care system, but we would take Jaon back in a heartbeat. It took a week for us to open our home. At that time, he had been placed in three homes because of his behavior.

Rickey took to parenting naturally. He had the experiences that came with growing up in a loving household, but those experiences were not something that I had during my upbringing. I remember being worried about what I considered dumb stuff. I was worried that I wouldn't be a good mother. I'm confident now that I'm a great mother, though I'm always open to learning more.

My first experience as a parent came when Jaon was a baby. At that time, Rickey and I were going through what I now consider to be our rebellion and challenge period. I was not completely ready to be a parent due to lessons I had yet to learn—both personally and in my relationship with Rickey. By the time Rickey and I were able to work out our differences and get back together, we had come to a place where we were a stable family. When we brought Jaon back into our family, we were able to welcome him into a healthy environment that was appropriately focused on him. Our home had become a place that enabled him to be a child and to learn and grow.

Some of the things I wish parents knew and took advantage of when it comes to creating a child-friendly home are the educational opportunities, nurturing, and support that can be found. Rickey and I attended parenting classes, seminars, and more, which helped us build a stable family environment. In addition to the courses that we took, we also had Rickey's mother, Jonet, who taught us how to be a good parent as she fussed about keeping socks on baby Jaon's feet when he was out of the house. It was clear that Jonet loved him and felt as if he was her grandson, not a foster child. She provided additional lessons on parenting and was an invaluable source of information and support.

HIS OTHER MOM

Throughout the time that we fostered Jaon, his biological mom was always checking in on him. I took him to see her every week for a few months, a routine that I was very supportive of. But she was young, and one day her phone number changed, and she never called me again. I did not hear from her until a court date was scheduled for the termination of parental rights.

We were caught up in the court system until Jaon was seven. Those years, and the accompanying stress and chaos, took a toll on our son. He had trouble understanding why he could not be with his biological mother, and I attempted to explain to him that she was going through a lot herself. Finally, the adoption was finalized.

After the adoption, his biological mother was doing better. She had three other children she was caring for, and she was living on her own with her fiancé. Late one night, while her fiancé was at work,

Donna was cooking food and somehow a fire broke out. She was able to get the two youngest children out of the house, but when she went back in for the oldest, she never came out, and both were lost in the fire.

Jaon's two youngest siblings survived the fire and were living with their father and grandfather. Within a year, a fire broke out at the grandfather's home. His two surviving siblings passed away in that fire. As you can see, my son has been through a lot in his young life.

I believe it bothers him that he did not get to know his mother or his siblings and that he does not know who his biological father is. When he attended a dinner with his maternal grandmother and aunts, his only question was, "Who is my father?" but they did not know. He did learn that due to her generous spirit and love for others, Donna was an organ donor and through donation saved six lives.

A MESSAGE TO MY SON

For all my time here on Earth, I will give praises to God for giving me such an amazing son as Jaon. He is now an adolescent and I want to help prepare him for the world I was unprepared for. God is the answer. We succeed as we trust in Him. Jaon is well on his way. People have told me that he has Shekinah glory.

I want my son to know that he has enormous power. He can do whatever he wants to do with his life. My message to him is also my message to you: Focus on the love you have in your world and use that love to overcome any fears you may have along the journey of life. The people who love you, love you more than you know. There is no limit to the heights you can reach when that kind of love surrounds you.

One of the most powerful kinds of love that I have witnessed is the love between my son and my husband. My husband is an excellent cook, and he used to play football. Jaon told me that he wants to be a football player and a chef. He enjoys both activities and knows he can make a living doing what he loves. I believe he has taken after his father. The two of them spend hours watching football games and cooking shows with expert chefs, and they have a great relationship.

The lesson that can be learned from their relationship is that fathers are blessings. By extension, parents are blessings—especially when love is at the center of the household. I learned about family values and how to construct healthy environments in school, and my husband learned the same principles at home. Because we knew what a healthy family looked like, we were able to apply those principles to the failures and struggles in our relationship, which allowed us to build a stable home life. We then invited Jaon into that healthy environment. By combining our progress, book knowledge, and experiences, we were able to provide a foundation for our decision-making in the home. Seek the same for your world. Learn, seek the truth, and decide.

CHAPTER 7

The Pattern of Marriage

I started going to church with Rickey when I was sixteen years old, in addition to attending a different church with my mom. After two years of attending both churches, I decided to stick with Rickey's church. I diligently attended until I was in my early thirties. I got a little lax for a few years after that. When I woke up after my ruptured brain aneurysm in 2020, I heard a male voice telling me, "Listen to God and Jesus." I believe it was the Holy Spirit speaking to me. The voice was clear, and I remember looking around because it sounded like a man was on the right side of the room. After that experience, I knew for sure that I would go back to church as soon as I was physically able to.

I did not grow up attending church. As a result, I feel like there are lessons I missed that I am only learning now. The biggest focus of my life now is to help others learn early on about the benefits of God.

My son is my first and primary student. My goal is to make sure he understands who God is, so he doesn't have to learn as many life lessons the hard way as I did.

I will be the first to admit that I am a believer in training. I don't know all there is to know about the Bible, but what I do know is that I must train up my child in the way he should go. I want to ensure that Jaon knows that he is loved by his parents and by an omnipotent God. Recently, I have been interested in how the pattern of my marriage demonstrates the love of God in a real way. The love that my husband and I share is the greatest testament to God's love, His mercy, and His commitment to caring.

GOD AND THE BIBLE

The pattern of the Bible is unconditional love. It's also the guide for a healthy marriage. The lesson is that marriage reveals how God structures relationships. In the union between God and the Church, two lessons are present. First, you can see the sacrifice made by someone who loves you. God sent His Son to die for our sins so that His sacrifice would be counted to us as righteousness. The second lesson is found in communion with God being a part of His body of believers. This body is more than just a corporation.

It is a living and breathing entity, inhaling the breath of life, and exhaling the good news of Christ.

Marriage reflects the second lesson. The Bible states that a husband and wife shall "be one flesh" (Genesis 2:24) when they are joined together. The second lesson is unity. A husband's care and protection and a wife's support and nurturing all point toward the power and grace that God demonstrated in sending His Son to Earth.

MY HUSBAND, MY SUPERMAN

My husband and I are so in love. I tell him every day, "I love you so much, Superman!"

The benefits of an active husband and father cannot be overstated. My husband is not only my superman in marriage, but he is also my superman in partnership, making up for where I feel I am deficient. He pulls his weight. And sometimes, he pulls mine as well. My former views of what a man should be are blown away as I see how he loves me, provides for me beyond just the financial aspect, and represents God in our home. I could not ask for a more special union, and I am happy that I can now recognize it with more sober and attentive eyes than ever before.

My husband moves us forward without worry so that we can take the needed steps and find the peace to work together. Our partnership is a great example of what God does for the Church and each one of us. The grace that God showed us in Christ has continued to manifest as calm and intentional growth in our lives. I have power through God, and I make sure to go through Him instead of leaning on my own understanding. My husband is very funny and has taught our son to be funny as well. Their jokes helped me ward off depression when I got out of the hospital in 2020.

My husband grew up attending church and learning lessons about the Bible, so he is able to teach Jaon the things that he knows about the Bible. The lessons that he shares are often practical and full of love and power. My husband instructs my son and I listen in and gain just about as much information as my son does while admiring the knowledge that my husband possesses.

If you pay attention and commit yourself to the still, small voice of progress, kindness, and faith, you will find the greatest blessings and power. It is wonderful when you find those blessings mirrored within your home. "A family that prays together stays together," as they say. I would add that a family that mirrors kindness and faith reflects God's love. The world certainly needs this type of mirror and reflection. Searching for and accepting this gift of kindness and faith is critical to the health and well-being of your family.

FAMILY AND INFLUENCE

My family is stronger as we seek God and His righteousness. I want my son to know better than I did that we are not alone, and that power exists and it's available to us for our use. You can accomplish anything you set your mind to because your success is preordained; your path is set. You must only choose to walk on that path and persist in that faith and practice.

The primary message of the Church, as an institution, is one of mutual support. Being able to talk to God about the things I want in life, the things that happen in my life, and the person I want to be is an experience I welcome. I am in a women's group at church, and I remember a discussion we had about healing and God's opportunity to work through my experience in order to reach others with the gospel of Christ. I know that I can rely on my church family to support me when I share my testimony. And I know I can rely on God to lead me and order my steps.

The more I learn about myself and God, the more determined I am to live for Him. I am also learning how to maintain my growth and development. I can apply what I've learned through my personal experiences, professional training, and become a new person as I move toward my aspirations. I can apply what I've learned through my personal experiences and professional training and become a new person as I move toward my aspirations. I am not alone in this. I have my church family to support and propel me along the way, and I can depend on God to guide and strengthen me.

I know that God is on my side! I continue with my daily affirmations and prayer, from which I have both asked and received. I have experienced God's favor firsthand. I remember receiving my favorite car, a white Range Rover, after much prayer and belief. I recall when the doctor told my husband that I would need to use a walker when I got out of the hospital, but instead, I walked out without a problem. Even when I had to step away from my business, it continued to flow seamlessly—even growing through the rest of the year! I know that my blessings are beyond the material, as I am awakening to the power that God has granted me through my family and my church home. I am excited to see what He works within me next.

CHAPTER 8

Love and Power in the Church

THE LESSONS

Struggles, challenges, or difficulties do not have to define you. God has more in store for you than you realize. You can move forward and integrate the realities of your life without becoming stuck. I would like to share some of the lessons that I have learned throughout my journey forward.

I had a rough time growing up as a kid, and I witnessed many forms of challenges, pains, and disappointment. I taught myself how to be independent and never give up. I tried to ensure that I wouldn't face disappointments like I did when I was a kid, but I never grew close to God like I was supposed to. If people ask me, I will say that the path I trod wasn't apparent to me at that time. I was stuck in ruts and hurdles, but all of it makes up who I am today. Day to day, I immersed myself in work, but I was sick of hearing myself complain about being stressed and tired. I then learned about affirmations, and I loved them! I have notebooks that I wrote affirmations in when I woke up in the mornings.

Whenever I wanted something, I would say a daily affirmation about it. After all, isn't that what faith is about? As Paul taught, "We having the same spirit of faith, according as it is written, I believed, and therefore have I spoken; we also believe, and therefore speak" (2 Corinthians 4:13, BRG). We speak through our belief, and our belief is molded by what we say.

"Faith is the substance of things hoped for, the evidence of things not seen" (Hebrews 11:1, NKJV). Every day for two years, I said a daily affirmation about my favorite white Range Rover, and I eventually got it in February 2020. In the Bible, Jesus Himself taught: "If you have faith as small as a mustard seed, you can say to this mulberry tree, 'Be uprooted and planted in the sea,' and it will obey you." (Luke 17:6, NIV). Affirmations help me to grow and practice my faith.

LOVE

My life has been a search for love. My father was physically abusive, my stepfather was sexually abusive, and I broke my husband's heart due to not knowing what to expect from a man or how to appreciate one. The lessons of love must be applied to your life every day. My story today is a story of the blessings of complete love.

As a child, my grandmother, Ganny, would sometimes take Latrisha and me to her church. When I was sixteen years old, I found myself occasionally visiting a church named New Dimensions Ministries. Things were back to normal at home, and I was living with my mother again. When I visited the church, I met with Bishop Randall L. House Sr. and Co-Pastor Betty House who headed the church and are the great uncle and aunt of my husband, Rickey. I didn't know much about the Scriptures at that time, but I loved what I was learning in church. However, I think the fact that my mother never went to church affected me because, after a while, I found myself gradually drifting away from God. I tried to justify my actions by making excuses every time someone addressed me about church.

I didn't learn as much about God as my husband did. I doubted whether I knew God at all because how would it be possible to know Him if I didn't make myself familiar with the Scriptures? At first, my excuse was that I needed time to rest because I was always working. That excuse continued until I stopped going to church for two years. I was willing to let go of the gospel because I felt other things were more important. What I was telling myself sounded right, so I went less and less. I believed in Christianity because my husband is a Christian. He was familiar with the religion and had more knowledge than I did. Rickey grew up learning and studying the Word of God, and he developed an intimate relationship with God, which I didn't have at that point. My husband never liked that I was drifting away from God when I stopped going to church, but I have learned that if love could be defined, it would be described as patience. My husband was patient with me. And although he showed me that he didn't like the fact that I was preventing myself from getting to know God, he has always been patient with me.

Eventually, things began to change. I had questions and I was curious. When I found myself staying home to rest instead of going to church, I realized that I was not the only one fighting battles when it came to faith. It seemed to me that lots of people hated Christians, which inspired some of my questions. Why would anyone ever think that Christianity is just to exploit people, especially the less privileged? I feel sad whenever I see posts on social media condemning Christians. One day, I stumbled on a post that said, "Christianity is just another way to bring Black people back into slavery." I could not understand that post. I had many questions that I could not answer because I didn't have much understanding of God. Now, whenever I stumble upon posts directed against Christians, I realize that just like myself, there are many people out there who perish because they lack basic knowledge.

Since waking up in the hospital, I have begun to hear and feel God. I know that He has saved me and kept me here for a purpose. Knowing that I am still here and surrounded by people who love me reminds me that God loves me in many ways.

POWER

Before my aneurism, I did not understand how life worked or how the universe functioned. When I woke up at a rehabilitation hospital, I got close to God. Reading was a challenge for me so I could not read the Bible. I prayed, then I watched one of my three favorite pastors, and I have been motivated to learn more about God and Jesus ever since.

This brings me to Ephesians 3:20 (NIV): "Now unto him that is able to do immeasurably more than we ask or imagine, according to his power that is within us." I don't remember why this Bible verse kept coming into my head, but I was amused by it and liked it. I wrote the Scripture on my morning affirmation page. I knew that my heart was drawn to that Scripture for some reason. While everyone was preparing for the 2020 new year, I found myself going to church again. It was interesting because I went to my church to figure out what they had up for the new year, as they would always post Scriptures that people could affirm every day. I was excited, a big smile formed on my face, and my heart leaped for joy when I noticed that my church had posted the same Bible verse that had lingered on my mind for a long time: "2020: The year of plenty. (Ephesians 3:20)." I posted the verse on my Facebook page and when I saw my church posting the verse again, I felt so much excitement. I had newfound faith in the Word of God as I entered the new year. I knew the Scripture had a deeper meaning, and I was convinced that the Bible was truly directed toward me.

I am working daily to clarify my message. My affirmations were only the beginning for me. I used to say them and make them happen, but not acknowledge the source of the blessings I received. When I started the practice of using affirmations to manifest results in my life, I quickly saw that they were working, but I didn't make them about God. I thought that I had my own power. I was confused. That was at the time when I was not sure of God. And, for a time, Satan used my experiences with affirmations to convince me that I didn't need God. But reading Ephesians 3:20-21 (ESV) puts our abundant blessings into perspective: "Now to him who is able to do far more abundantly than all that we ask or think, according to the power at work within us, *to him be glory in the church and in Christ Jesus throughout all generations, forever and ever.*" Though I did not understand it at the time, I know now that the wonderful results I manifested in my life were truly support from God and His presence; my affirmations worked because I was activating the biblical principle "ask and receive." I did not understand that they happened due to support from God and His presence, and I did not know that I was activating a biblical principle to ask and receive. I know now that God is present in my thoughts, my desires, and my decision-making. He is all in all.

In my opinion, based upon my experiences, God gets almost zero praise when we get what we want. At certain points in my life, I certainly didn't give Him any. I rarely hear people thank or give God praise when they achieve the things they want. But if these things don't come from God, then where do they come from? If we are not careful—and do not recognize the true source of our blessings—we might find ourselves receiving our desires from the enemy who is always prowling, aware of our carnal desires, and ready to use them to move us further away from God. The Bible tells us that all good things come from the Lord, but if we do not include Him in our plans and do not give Him any praise or glory for our blessings, then we risk relying solely on ourselves. And relying solely on myself is not a place I ever want to be.

When I do rely on God, I find it hard to say whether He is leading my desires or just responding to them. Either way, my life is made better. I am convinced that true partnership provides an example of love, and an attractive love draws others to Christ. It reminds me of my business. The same love that takes care of people in my business is the love shared in my family and within the Church. I can truly say that love is One. God is love. If we make Him our focus, He will prosper us.

Why waste time brooding over things that we have little or no control over? It's pointless. After making daily affirmations for two years about my dream car, I got it. The same process works for other desires in my life. I realized that I don't need to stress myself out trying to discover what the purpose of my life is; all I need is to be happy. And once I tasted happiness in the context of love, my experience was enhanced. Things were good before my aneurism, but life has been even better since I woke up. Each day, I am returning to myself. I had to learn how to read and speak again, just like I did before. Yet, I refuse to return to the experience of life I had prior. I am committed to seeing life in more vibrant colors, loving more, and experiencing the benefits of a personal relationship with God.

LAW OF ATTRACTION

When I learned about affirmations in 2017, I loved them and entered a state of creation! I had books that I would write affirmations in whenever I woke up in the morning. Whenever I wanted something, I would say a daily affirmation about it. I was not talking to God or going to church at that point, and at first, I didn't recognize the source of the good things I was receiving. In 2018, I started to purchase my business. In March 2020, I got my favorite vehicle: a white Range Rover. My family and I have twenty-one acres of beautiful land. I was on the news and discussed mental health and adolescents. I trained my business team about herbs and mental health. My husband and I went on a cruise with my mother and stepfather, and about two weeks later, I had a ruptured brain aneurysm. I was in a medically induced coma for about a month!

What is the Law of Attraction?

The alluring, magnetic power of the universe appears in everyone and everything through the law of attraction. The law is a manifestation of the creative force of the universe. Even the law of gravity is included in the law of attraction. Thoughts, ideas, people, situations, circumstances, and the things you think about are all attracted and bound by this law. The law of attraction can be harnessed for producing your ideal world by using your mind, thoughts, and imagination. It connects you with others who share your views, ideas, topics, and the circumstances that you think about regularly.

What is the Common Understanding of the Law of Attraction?

The saying that "like attracts like" and the idea that focusing on positive or negative thoughts can bring about positive or negative results are forms of the concept known as the Law of Attraction. The Law of Attraction, often known as New Thought, is based on the notion that people and their thoughts are pure energy that attracts similar energies. While this remark appears straightforward and rational, the spiritual power underlying it has to be investigated.

While the term Law of Attraction was already used in the late 1800s and promoted in psychological and spiritual circles, it acquired prominence after Oprah Winfrey, Ellen DeGeneres, and Larry King promoted it in the 2006 film *The Secret*. According to the film and book of the same name, "Everything one desires or needs can be satisfied by believing in an outcome, repeatedly thinking about it, and sustaining good emotional states to 'attract' the desired outcome." While many dispute whether or not the Law of Attraction is true, one thing is certain: the concept of possessing exceptional mental abilities is not new. The following is mentioned in the Bible:

"Now, the serpent was more subtle than any beast of the field which the LORD God had made. And he said unto the woman, 'Yea, hath God said, Ye shall not eat of every tree of the garden?' And the woman said unto the serpent, 'We may eat of the fruit of the trees of the garden: But of the fruit of the tree which is in the midst of the garden, God hath said, 'Ye shall not eat of it, neither shall ye touch it, lest ye die.' And the serpent said unto the woman, 'Ye shall not surely die: For God doth know that in the day ye eat thereof, then your eyes shall be opened, and ye shall be as gods, knowing good and evil.'" (Genesis 3:1-5, KJV)

Here, Satan tempted Eve by claiming to have superhuman insight. But, of course, we learn soon after that this "knowledge" was a scourge that killed humanity (Romans 5:12-21). So, with only the power of their minds, people have the ability to produce supernatural change outside of their direct physical control.

"Whenever you speak negatively, you create a conflict between the good and bad seed that is in your heart."
—Creflo A. Dollar

THE POWER OF CONFESSION AND AUTHORITY

We are ruled by our words and our words are determined by our thinking. Our entire lives are the result of words shouted over us or said by us. As Charles Capps points out, "Words are the most powerful thing in the universe... Words are containers. They contain faith, or fear, and they produce after their kind." The words we say are determined by our thoughts, but our thoughts and actions can also be changed through the words we choose to say (this is one reason affirmations are so powerful). Bill

Winston said this: "When your beliefs change, your behavior changes, which ultimately changes the results you are getting in life. Transform your thinking, transform your life." And Reverend Ike Legacy put it this way: "Whatever you say you are, you will become that. Whatever you say you are, you will remain that."

Confession works in the same way. There are two types of confession. The first is the confession of one's faults and sins in order to be forgiven—Just as 1 John 1:9 (KJV) says, "If we confess our sins, He is faithful and just to forgive us our sins and to cleanse us of all unrighteousness."

The second is the confession of God's Word over our lives to activate His Word in our lives. (Proverbs 18:21 [NIV] says, "Death and life are in the power of the tongue, and those who love it will eat its fruit.")

The second confession is more than just reciting God's Word. You must first get the Word into your soul through meditation in order for it to come alive and become real to you. (I've found meditation to be a powerful tool for change. In the words of Bill Winston, "Meditation is the way to secure your future without struggle.")

Many people confess the Word to imitate what others are saying and to sound and appear spiritual, but they have no success. That is because the Word they are confessing has not yet taken root within them. As Creflo A. Dollar says, "God desires that we position ourselves to hear His voice so we can receive the Word that will change our lives forever." To be in a place where we can receive the Word, we need to make time for it. That being said, true confession begins in the heart. Please keep in mind that humans have two mouths: an inner and an exterior mouth. Before your confession can produce for you, the inner and outward mouths must concur. Your inner mouth is the voice of your reasoning and thoughts, and what you think about the most becomes your belief. If you keep believing you're cursed, you'll eventually say it out loud. As a result, you will attract people and circumstances that make your life seem cursed! At one point or another, we've all said it to ourselves. Friends, be careful what you say because our words have power over us.

Your inner self is the first thing you should work on. You must instill an abundance of God's Word and promises into yourself, then they will burst from your tongue and change your world. Only words can reconstruct the world we live in because they created it.

Filling our lives with God's Word and promises will give our minds purpose. And as Reverend Ike Legacy said, "Give your mind a purpose, and it will find all of the necessary ways and means of accomplishing the purpose you give it."

I encourage you to return to the basics and begin to feed yourself with the Word of God until it naturally flows off your tongue. I dwell on Scriptures rather than memorize them. The Word becomes alive in my spirit and memory with continuous concentration. When I pray in tongues, I allow Scriptures to pass through my head, enriching both my mind and my emotions in the process. To live a triumphant life, friends, you must pay careful attention to what you focus on in order to govern your confession, for our confessions rule us.

THE AUTHORITY

We must remember that as we travel through these challenging times, Jesus Christ has granted us His authority, and our confession has a direct bearing on how we act in that authority.

"When Jesus came to the region of Caesarea Philippi, he asked his disciples, 'Who do people say the Son of Man is?' They replied, 'Some say John the Baptist; others say Elijah; and still others, Jeremiah or one of the prophets.' 'But what about you?' he asked. 'Who do you say I am?' Simon Peter answered, 'You are the Messiah, the Son of the living God.' Jesus replied, 'Blessed are you, Simon son of Jonah, for this was not revealed to you by flesh and blood, but by my Father in heaven. And I tell you that you are Peter, and on this rock I will build my church, and the gates of Hades will not overcome it. I will give you the keys of the kingdom of heaven; whatever you bind on earth will be bound in heaven, and whatever you loose on earth will be loosed in heaven" (Matthew 16:13-19, NIV).

The Church was built on solid ground! The revelation that Jesus Christ is the Son of God is the rock of revelation. There are numerous things to take away from this passage of Scripture, but what I want you to notice is that by confessing that Jesus Christ is the Son of God, you are gaining access to Christ's very power!

"Then, He called His twelve disciples together and gave them power and authority over all demons, and to cure diseases. He sent them to preach the kingdom of God and to heal the sick" (Luke 9:1-2, NKJV). The strength comes from the person who is rooting for us. We are disciples...under his authority! When Jesus sent out the seventy disciples, they all came back in one piece, saying, "Lord, even the demons are subject to us in Your name." (Luke 10:17, NKJV).

"And He said to them, 'I saw Satan fall like lightning from heaven. Behold, I give you the authority to trample on serpents and scorpions, and overall, the power of the enemy, and nothing shall by any means hurt you'" (Luke 10:18-19, NKJV).

All of the enemy's strength has been entrusted to us by Jesus Christ. We have authority if He has given us the keys to the kingdom. Authorization is granted through keys. We have permission to enter and exit, open and close, lock and unlock the door. On behalf of the one who gave us the keys, we are authorized to conduct business or kingdom transactions!

Many of us are terrified right now. We are terrified of the current state of affairs in the world. We're pleading with the Lord for assistance, but I am convinced that God can and will bring a startling awakening to the globe. He will, I believe, use the chaos to bring many people to know Him as their personal Lord and Savior. I also feel that as a Church, we ought to go to the Lord and seek illumination rather than merely intervention. My prayer is: "Lord, please shine a light on what You're doing right now. Make the valuable things we need to be concerned about more visible. Give us insight into how we, your Church, can be Your hands and feet in this hour. Show us how to exercise our authority through confession, prayer, and community service. Lord, enlighten us with Your peace that exceeds all comprehension."

Don't allow the adversary to steal your tranquility, beloved! Even in the midst of the world's current instability, Christ reigns supreme! That is something we must remember! You still have control over all of the enemy's works. Keep your attention on Him and allow Him to demonstrate His peace and abundance to you! Refuse to allow the enemy to take your peace by standing in the authority Christ has given you!

You are a child of the Most High, and you have the power to conquer any difficulties.

Words have a lot of creative power. God's spoken word created the entire cosmos and everything in it. As believers who have been made righteous by faith, we have been given the same authority as God. We can speak healing, deliverance, success, or anything else we desire into our lives. On the other hand, we can say bad things that cause us troubles and keep us trapped. As a result, we must use caution when we speak as our words can either propel us forward or set us back. When Christians realize this, they will be able to soar above any power of limitation.

CHAPTER 9
Wealth and Riches

Money is a generally accepted, recognized, and centralized medium of exchange in an economy that is used to facilitate transactional trade for goods and services. Under this simple definition, one is wealthy if they have enough money to pay for good quality food, adequate clothing, and shelter for protection from the weather. When I was growing up, my family had money difficulties and didn't consistently have enough money in the home to get by. Rickey and I continued to have difficulties with money. We moved into an apartment together. I worked in fast food, at a department store, and I went to college. Because of his size, Rickey had difficulties getting and keeping jobs. With money running low, I stole money, clothes, and food from my jobs. When we needed money to pay bills, I learned about donating plasma. I was able to get enough money to pay the electric bill, put gas in the car, and buy us some food. A young lady that lived near us suggested that I make extra money as a stripper. Yes, I was an exotic dancer for three months when I was nineteen years old. Looking back, it is so clear that those things were not working for us.

I learned how to trust God to take care of us. We pray to God, we do our part, and we have faith that we will be prosperous and wealthy. A quote I love from Creflo A. Dollar goes like this: "Faith is a practical expression of the confidence we have in God and His Word, while trust is a practical expression of our commitment to God and His Word." We pray and believe God will bless us, then we act based on that trust.

My family and I have been blessed in ways that we never expected. One affirmation I would say was, "Money flows to us and we are open to giving and receiving." That certainly came true!

As Christians, it is important to understand our material wealth from God's point of view. Apostle John writes in 3 John 1:2 (ESV), "Beloved, I pray that all may go well with you and that you may be in good health, as it goes well with your soul." you may flourish in all things and be in good health, just as your soul prospers." Wealth entails having enough tangible belongings to live and thrive as a human being made in God's image, as well as, having a specific heart attitude toward God's purpose of possessions.

Viewing your financial prosperity as a blessing from God to be used in ways that praise Him is appropriate. But when that same money isolates you from God and stifles your spiritual growth, it's a very different story. Don't become arrogant. Work hard and achieve success in life, but don't consider yourself superior to others because of your financial possessions. Moses says in Deuteronomy 8:18 (NIV), "But remember the Lord your God, for it is he who gives you the ability to produce wealth, and so confirms his covenant, which he swore to your ancestors, as it is today."

Don't put your hope in your wealth. "Cast only a glance at riches, and they are gone, because they will surely sprout wings and fly off to the sky like an eagle," says Proverbs 23:5 (NIV). A strong career or business with consistent revenue can appear today and vanish tomorrow. Be rich in good deeds. A good deed is a selfless act of service to another person. The fruit of your salvation in Jesus Christ is doing good things for others. Ephesians 2:10 (NIV) says, "For we are God's handiwork, created in Christ Jesus to do good works, which God prepared in advance for us to do."

CAN YOU BE RICH AND BE A CHRISTIAN?

Can a Christian be wealthy while remaining a true Christian? After all, Jesus was impoverished, and the apostles were poor. Jesus ordered the rich young ruler to sell everything he owned and donate the proceeds to the poor.

But it is important to remember that Jesus also had wealthy friends who assisted Him financially (Luke 8:3). He didn't tell them to give all of their money away and live in poverty. So, how should we view riches?

According to the Bible, wealth is like fire, good yet hazardous. Because everyone perceives the good, the Bible warns us of four main dangers associated with wealth. The first danger is the ambition to become wealthy (1 Timothy 6:10). The second danger is putting one's confidence in wealth rather than God (Luke 12:16-21). The third danger is treating money as your god, despite the fact that no man can serve two masters (Matthew 6:24). The fourth danger is using your money to oppress others (James 2:6, Isaiah 3:15, Amos 2:6-7). Wise men are wary of the temptations that accompany prosperity.

A man or woman can be wealthy while also being a member of God's people. Abraham was a rich man. But our life goal cannot be to get rich if we are to be true Christians. The Creator's most important objective for man is to glorify and enjoy Him forever, not to get rich. One can be wealthy as a Christian, but one cannot worship both God and money at the same time. True Christians seek eternal life more than they seek riches.

UNDERSTANDING GOD'S PURPOSES FOR MONEY IN CHRISTIANITY

Money is a major source of tension in today's marriages, even in Christian relationships. Everyone has different ideas about how their money should be spent. But as Christians, we need to realize that everything we have comes from God and belongs to Him. In order to be good stewards of the money God has entrusted to us, we must first learn about and comprehend God's purposes for money. Knowing and applying God's purposes for money results in financial freedom. An inaccurate view of God's purposes for money results in financial enslavement and many other consequences that can harm your marriage, health, and faith.

A man with financial freedom can build his job around his family; a man without financial freedom is often forced to build his family around his job. God desires that we be financially independent so that we can serve Him better. In the words of Pastor Joel Osteen, "Friend, God has a fatted calf, a place of abundance for you. He is not limited by your circumstances, by how you were raised, or by what you don't have. He is limited by what you're believing." God wants to bless us with prosperity once we get our priorities straight.

According to God's Word, there are fundamental purposes for money: to provide for basic needs, to confirm direction, to give to those in need, and to illustrate God's power and care in provision. Understanding these purposes allows you to comprehend how money relates to God's work in your life and in your community.

BIBLICAL PRINCIPLES FOR FINANCIAL SUCCESS AND PEACE OF MIND

1. **Surround yourself with fiscally responsible people.** "Walk with the wise and become wise, for a companion of fools suffers harm" (Proverbs 13:20, NIV). It is difficult to cut ties with people, but if you are struggling financially, it may be necessary to distance yourself from financially irresponsible people so you can get your finances in order. God may

use a friend, a teacher, a parent, or a preacher to convey His message of truth. Their words may come as a warning, a blessing, or as a prophetic truth about our lives. Whether we choose to hear it or ignore it depends on us. The words from Dr. Peter Messiah and my business coach, Aprille Franks, have been blessings in a million ways to me and my family. Because of learning from their wisdom, my family ascended to a higher level.

2. **Gain financial knowledge.** "Therefore, my people will go into exile for lack of understanding; those of high rank will die of hunger and the common people will be parched with thirst" (Isaiah 5:13, NIV). One of the most crucial biblical financial principles for any Christian who wishes to be financially stable or frugal is to learn about personal finance.

3. **Self-control and discipline.** "*There is* desirable treasure, And oil in the dwelling of the wise, But a foolish man squanders it" (Proverbs 21:20, NKJV). This doesn't mean that you should become a hoarder or have a poverty mindset, it just means that you should

be more intentional with your spending. In addition, your overriding purpose should be to honor God with your money.

4. **Sacrifice.** Making sacrifices is one of the most essential biblical financial teachings. Take a close look at how you manage your money. Is there going to be a sacrifice? Are you willing to give up a few items in exchange for a better financial situation? "Will a man rob God? Yet, you are robbing me. But you say, 'How have we robbed you?' In your tithes and contributions. You are cursed with a curse, for you are robbing me, the whole nation of you. Bring the full tithe into the storehouse, that there may be food in my house. And thereby put me to the test, says the Lord of hosts, if I will not open the windows of heaven for you and pour down for you a blessing until there is no more need. I will rebuke the devourer for you so that it will not destroy the fruits of your soil, and your vine in the field shall not fail to bear, says the Lord of hosts. Then, all nations will call you blessed, for you will be a land of delight, says the Lord of hosts" (Malachi 3:8-12, NKJV).

5. **Honesty.** "For the love of money is a root of all kinds of evil. Some people, eager for money, have wandered from the faith and pierced themselves with many griefs" (1 Timothy 6:10, NIV). Honesty always triumphs. If you operate a business, always attempt to deal honestly with your customers and vendors and never compromise your integrity.

6. **Financial planning.** "Be sure you know the condition of your flocks, give careful attention to your herds" (Proverbs 27:23, NIV). You can't have a sound financial foundation unless you plan. Planning keeps you financially on track and prevents you from making life-changing blunders. Begin by assessing your current situation. Understand the state of your money, create financial goals, then devise a plan to improve your financial situation.

CHAPTER 10

Continuous Learning

Almost dying has a way of forcing you to think about what is most important in life. Since my ruptured brain aneurysm, I've struggled with many difficult questions and come to a few powerful conclusions. My story wouldn't be complete if I didn't share these final lessons with you.

When 2020 started, my life was amazing. I went on a cruise, I got my white Range Rover, and my business was growing quickly. I was featured on the news talking about adolescent mental health and my husband and I were enjoying a healed marriage, free from our previous relational problems. My son was growing into a great young man, and I couldn't have asked for more.

Then, out of nowhere, an aneurysm in my brain ruptured and turned my world upside down. I came home from the hospital after six weeks, but the healing was far from complete. In fact, I was just beginning the journey back to functionality.

At the time of this writing, it has been almost two years since the incident and I am still healing from aphasia, seizures, high blood pressure, and fibroids. The most challenging part of it all is the aphasia, which makes it more difficult for me to understand speech or speak clearly. What keeps me going is faith. I *know* that I will not only get better but that I will be better than I was before!

To cement this belief, I say affirmations. I call them affirmations, but really what they are is what God has given each of us: authority, confessions, and power to declare things in His name. One of the greatest lessons I learned from this health trial of mine is that God wants us to move forward. Satan wants us to stay focused on the negative parts of our past. We defeat Satan when we move forward. We must refuse to look back. We must look forward and press ahead!

Another lesson I learned from my trial is that moving forward is a choice. We have everything we need to move forward right now. God has us here for a reason! My best days are ahead of me, and so are yours! Your best days are not lost in your past, they are waiting to be discovered in your future.

Having faith will help you realize those bright days ahead. I love this quote from Pastor Joel Osteen:

"Dare to have a big vision for an abundant life, and trust God to bring it to pass. You don't have to figure out how it's going to happen. All you have to do is believe. One touch of God's favor can bring any dream to pass." On another occasion, Joel Osteen said, "If you're not expecting increase, promotion, or good breaks, you're not releasing your faith. Faith is what causes God to act."

Faith can move mountains. Whatever challenges you are facing today, I know that you can be victorious. The enemy of our souls tried to stop me by getting me to give up hope. He tried to convince me that my life would never be as good as it once was and that my experience will forever cripple me. But thanks to God, I know that I am headed to my next level. What I have gone through is an upgrade, and if I can be made better by my trial, then you can be made better by yours. To the end of moving forward and reaching the next wonderful level of life that God has made possible for you, here are four practical tips to keep in mind that have helped me and my family:

1. **Make decisions with God's guidance.** Decisions—even small ones—can drastically change the course of our lives. Take time to consult your all-knowing Creator when making them. Seek God's advice and wisdom

through prayer. Another place we can find guidance from God is in His Word (the Bible). The Bible can teach us through giving us practical counsel, by inviting the Holy Spirit into our lives, and by teaching us about ourselves.

"We think of the Bible perhaps as some collection of theological fairy tales, but the Bible is the greatest book of self-image psychology ever written." —Reverend Ike Legacy.

2. **Get rid of negative thoughts.** Negative thoughts that make you doubtful, anxious, or afraid are not from God. Regularly take inventory of your thoughts, identify the negative ones, and get rid of them. Negative thoughts won't help you to be better. When times get tough, everyone has to make a fundamental decision: complain or be grateful. In an environment where negative sentiment is rampant, the consequences of this decision are much greater. Complaining only attracts negative thoughts and people. Gratitude, on the other hand, creates the opportunity for the best thinking, actions, and results to emerge. We each have so much to be grateful

for. Bill Winston counsels: "God deliberately plants the righteous among the wicked to showcase his glory. Don't take the credit." Focus on everything you are grateful for, communicate those things, and open yourself up each day to the best possible opportunities God has given you.

Focusing on expanding your faith is another way to be positive. In the words of Charles Capps, "Faith and fear are opposite forces. Fear is the devil, and faith is of God." Doubt and negativity must be replaced with faith, for as Hebrews 11:1 (KJV) says, "Now faith is the substance of things hoped for, the evidence of things not seen."

When I was in the hospital after my brain aneurism, some people tried to help Rickey get ready for me to pass. Though well meaning, those people did not have faith! What kind of faith inspires you to get ready for the worst-case scenario? To get rid of negativity, Rickey had to stop talking to the people who weren't on his side.

3. **Take care of yourself.** Physical and mental health are important, and we should all take better care of ourselves. I took my functioning body and mind for granted until

my incident. That is something I'll never do again. Whether you're recovering from a physical trial like I am, wishing your mental health was better, or feeling like you can take on the world, take a step back and do things to take better care of yourself. Slow down and do what you need to do in order to get better or to prevent physical or mental collapse down the road. My message is to do the basics and understand them as the basics. Set your goals. Put them on a vision board to remind yourself of them daily. Take specific steps each day to reach those goals.

4. **Let God take care of your finances.** My family used to have many financial problems, and I know what it's like to be poor. I also know that you don't have to stay there. Philippians 4:19 (NKJV) reads, "And my God shall supply all your needs according to His riches in glory by Christ Jesus." If you put your trust in God, He will take care of your needs.

The idea of relying on the Lord for our daily bread is simple, yet it takes a lot of spiritual work to get to the place where you let God be your sole source of supply. God is the Creator of work, and as the Bible says,

"For even when we were with you, we were commanded you this: If anyone will not work, neither shall he eat" (2 Thessalonians 3:10, NKJV). However, God never intended for us to put our faith and hope in our labor alone. He also did not intend for you to turn anything else into your source—not your family, not your credit cards, and not the government. He is your source. So, lean on Him, and let Him do His thing.

A testimony is a powerful tool for sharing what God has done and continues to do in our lives. My testimony, though once shaken by a health crisis, is now firmer than ever. Like me, you don't have to be stuck where you are because no matter what difficulties you're facing, you can move through them and claim victory.

If I had to pick the single greatest lesson I learned through this recent trial and through the rest of the experiences I've had in life—both joyful and painful—I would say that I have learned who I am. I am a daughter of God. This spiritual identity gives me the strength and power to succeed in all I do. I know that God is near to me. As Reverend Ike Legacy said, "God is within you. God lives in you, through you and as you… God does not work for you from up in the sky. God works for you from within your very own mind."

Faith is powerful and can change your life! Before the aneurysm, I doubted God on various levels. I was no longer clear about His existence, and I wondered if my faith was for naught.

But after the aneurysm, I saw God working in my life. I learned to see my trial as another step in His perfect plan for me, and I know that He is there. I do my best to put Him first in my life, and I feel the Holy Spirit guiding me forward to a glorious future.

This is my testimony.

To you I say: have faith, keep moving forward, and we'll keep loving our lives together.

About the Author

Trina House, LPC, LPC-S is the CEO of The Prevention Center, a thriving counseling and holistic mental wellness practice in the greater Oklahoma City area.

House is a vocal advocate for mental health equality and culturally sensitive care. After obtaining her bachelor's degree, she realized a need for a different, more comprehensive approach to therapy, one designed to help people succeed in every area of their lives. She also recognized that it was necessary to connect clients with clinicians who looked like them, who could deeply connect with them, and who could understand exactly where they are.

House carried that vision with her for over a decade, and it has now become the foundation of The Prevention Center's revived mission. She and her team have developed a signature approach to mental wellness that blends clinical and holistic treatments to help clients feel, live, and do better.

Learn more at www.thepreventioncenterllc.org

CREATING DISTINCTIVE BOOKS
WITH INTENTIONAL RESULTS

We're a collaborative group of creative masterminds with a mission to produce high-quality books to position you for monumental success in the marketplace.

Our professional team of writers, editors, designers, and marketing strategists work closely together to ensure that every detail of your book is a clear representation of the message in your writing.

Want to know more?
Write to us at info@publishyourgift.com
or call (888) 949-6228

Discover great books, exclusive offers, and more at
www.PublishYourGift.com

Connect with us on social media

@publishyourgift

www.ingramcontent.com/pod-product-compliance
Lightning Source LLC
Chambersburg PA
CBHW071856070526
44583CB00016B/1716